CELEBRATING THE NAME RICHARD

Celebrating the Name Richard

Walter the Educator

Silent King Books a WhichHead Imprint

Copyright © 2024 by Walter the Educator

All rights reserved. No part of this book may be reproduced in any manner whatsoever without written permission except in the case of brief quotations embodied in critical articles and reviews.

First Printing, 2024

Disclaimer
This book is a literary work; poems are not about specific persons, locations, situations, and/or circumstances unless mentioned in a historical context. This book is for entertainment and informational purposes only. The author and publisher offer this information without warranties expressed or implied. No matter the grounds, neither the author nor the publisher will be accountable for any losses, injuries, or other damages caused by the reader's use of this book. The use of this book acknowledges an understanding and acceptance of this disclaimer.

dedicated to everyone with the first name of Richard

CONTENTS

Dedication v

One - Here's To Richard 1

Two - Shines So Bright 3

Three - Greatness 5

Four - Glory 7

Five - Legacy Is Found 9

Six - Oh, Richard 11

Seven - Speaks Of Grace 13

Eight - Every Hour 15

Nine - One-of-a-kind 17

Ten - All We Do 19

Eleven - Echoes 21

Twelve - Richard Gleams 23

Thirteen - Modern Streets 25

Fourteen - Timeless Measure	. . . .	27
Fifteen - Modern Richards	. . . .	29
Sixteen - Every Battle	. . . .	31
Seventeen - Cherished	. . . .	33
Eighteen - Name Fit For Kings	. . . .	35
Nineteen - Stands Tall	. . . .	37
Twenty - Time And Space	. . . .	39
Twenty-One - Symphony Of Strength	. . . .	41
Twenty-Two - Muse Of The Soul	. . . . . .	43
Twenty-Three - Never To Fade	. . . .	45
Twenty-Four - Resonates	. . . .	47
Twenty-Five - Forever Endure	. . . .	49
Twenty-Six - Dazzling Shade	. . . .	51
Twenty-Seven - Calm Of The Woods	. . . .	53
Twenty-Eight - No Need To Be Said	. . . . .	55
Twenty-Nine - Commands Respect	. . . . .	57
Thirty - Unique	. . . .	59
Thirty-One - Every Journey	. . . .	61
Thirty-Two - Timeless Choice	. . . .	63
Thirty-Three - Modern Days	. . . .	65

Thirty-Four - Never To Deceive 67

Thirty-Five - Raise Our Voices 69

Thirty-Six - Like Golden Sun 71

About The Creator 73

ONE

HERE'S TO RICHARD

Richard, like a regal sun, doth rise,
In the azure skies, his name implies,
A noble spirit, a steadfast heart,
In every quest, he plays his part.

Richard, with wisdom as his guide,
In every challenge, he stands with pride,
His laughter echoes through the halls,
Like a melody that never falls.

Richard, with a mind so sharp and bright,
He conquers darkness with his light,
In every tale, his name rings true,
A hero's journey, old and new.

Richard, a warrior of the pen,
His words ignite the hearts of men,
In every verse, a world unfolds,
Of mysteries and stories untold.

Richard, a friend, steadfast and true,
In every trial, he sees us through,
His kindness like a gentle breeze,
Bringing peace to troubled seas.

Richard, a name that stands the test of time,
In every rhythm, in every rhyme,
A name that echoes through history's halls,
A name that never fades, never falls.

So here's to Richard, with honor and grace,
In every challenge, in every race,
A name that shines, a name so bright,
A name that fills the world with light.

TWO

SHINES SO BRIGHT

Richard, a name that dances on the wind,
In every whisper, a tale begins,
A name that echoes through the ages past,
In every memory, it will forever last.

Richard, like a symphony in the night,
His presence fills the world with delight,
A name that carries strength and grace,
In every challenge, he finds his place.

Richard, with a spirit bold and free,
In every adventure, his soul roams free,
A name that paints the sky with hues,
In every moment, it brings good news.

Richard, a beacon in the darkest night,
His courage shines with radiant light,
A name that weaves through history's thread,
In every story, it's bravely led.

Richard, a friend with a heart so kind,
In every hardship, his warmth we find,
A name that brings joy and laughter near,
In every gathering, it's music to hear.

Richard, like a crown upon the earth,
In every kingdom, he's of noble birth,
A name that stands the test of time,
In every verse, it's a rhythm so prime.

So here's to Richard, a name so dear,
In every moment, it's crystal clear,
A name that holds a world of might,
In every heart, it shines so bright.

THREE

GREATNESS

 Richard, a name that echoes through time,
A moniker so noble, so truly sublime.
With each syllable, a tale unfolds,
Of courage, strength, and stories untold.
 In realms of old, Richard held sway,
A knight of valour, in battle's fray.
His name a banner, a mark of might,
In legends and lore, it shines so bright.
 Richard, a name that commands respect,
In history's annals, it stands erect.
From kings to poets, it finds its place,
A name of honor, of dignity and grace.
 In modern days, Richard stands strong,
A name of leaders, who right the wrong.
With wisdom and wit, they pave the way,
In boardrooms and beyond, they hold sway.

Richard, a name that carries a legacy,
Of conquerors and thinkers, bold and free.
In every Richard, a spirit untamed,
A legacy of greatness, forever unclaimed.
So here's to Richard, in all his glory,
A name that weaves an unforgettable story.
With each letter, a legacy is found,
In Richard, greatness will always abound.

FOUR

GLORY

Richard, a name that dances on the tongue,
A symphony of sounds, ancient and young.
In each syllable, a universe unfurls,
With echoes of triumphs and unfettered whirls.

In realms of yore, Richard reigned supreme,
A warrior's heart, a poet's dream.
His name a beacon, in history's flight,
A tapestry of valor, woven so bright.

Richard, a name that holds regal might,
In the tapestry of time, a guiding light.
From knights to scholars, it finds its place,
A name of honor, of dignity and grace.

In today's world, Richards stand tall,
With resilience and grace, they heed the call.
Their legacy echoes, in deeds untold,
In every Richard, a story to behold.

Richard, a name that weaves a tale,
Of bravery and kindness, beyond the pale.
In every letter, a legacy is found,
In Richard, greatness knows no bound.
So here's to Richard, in all his glory,
A name that echoes an eternal story.
With each heartbeat, a legacy unfurls,
In Richard, greatness spins and twirls.

FIVE

LEGACY IS FOUND

    Richard, a name that resonates with might,
A symphony of letters, bold and bright.
In every syllable, a tale takes flight,
Of chivalry, wisdom, and unyielding light.
    In ages past, Richard held his ground,
A name of kings, in history's profound.
His valorous spirit, a legend's embrace,
In chronicles of time, his name finds place.
    Richard, a name that echoes through the years,
In war and peace, it perseveres.
From battlefields to scholarly halls,
In Richard, greatness steadily calls.
    In this modern world, Richards stand tall,
With innovation and grace, they heed the call.
Their tenacity and spirit, a force to behold,
In every Richard, a story untold.

Richard, a name that carries a legacy,
Of conquerors and thinkers, bold and free.
In each letter, a saga is unfurled,
In Richard, greatness shapes the world.
So here's to Richard, in all his glory,
A name that weaves an enduring story.
In every heartbeat, a legacy is found,
In Richard, greatness knows no bound.

SIX

OH, RICHARD

Oh, Richard, a name of strength and might,
In the morning's first light, you shine so bright,
A name that echoes through the rolling hills,
And dances on the wind with joyous trills.

Richard, a name that stands with pride,
In every step, you never hide,
From challenges and triumphs, you emerge,
With courage and grace, you always surge.

In the tapestry of life, your name weaves,
A legacy of honor that never deceives,
In the symphony of existence, you play a part,
With a melody that resonates from heart to heart.

Richard, a name that carries history's weight,
Yet forges ahead, never a moment too late,
In every syllable, a story is told,
Of resilience and bravery, so bold.

So here's to Richard, in all his glory,
A name that embodies a timeless story,
Of valor, wisdom, and endless might,
A name that shines forever bright.

SEVEN

SPEAKS OF GRACE

Richard, a name like the gentle breeze,
Whispering through the ancient trees,
A name that holds the stars in its gaze,
And walks through life in a tranquil daze.

In the tapestry of existence, your name paints,
A portrait of serenity that never faints,
In the quiet moments, you find your peace,
And from chaos, you always find release.

Richard, a name that speaks of grace,
In every step, you find your place,
Amidst the chaos, you stand tall,
And in your presence, troubles fall.

In the symphony of life, your name rings clear,
A melody of hope that banishes fear,
In each verse, a tale of resilience and might,
A name that shines through the darkest night.

So here's to Richard, in all his calm,
A name that weaves its own soothing psalm,
Of tranquility, wisdom, and endless grace,
A name that time and space can never erase.

EIGHT

EVERY HOUR

Richard, a name that echoes through time,
A symphony of strength, a rhythm so prime,
In the dance of life, you waltz with grace,
Leaving an indelible mark in every space.

In the grand tapestry of human tale,
Your name weaves a saga, never frail,
With threads of valor and undying flame,
You etch your legacy, never the same.

Richard, a name that carries ancient lore,
A beacon of hope, a tempest's roar,
In every heartbeat, your name resounds,
A melody of resilience that surrounds.

In the orchestra of existence, you conduct,
A harmony of wisdom, never destruct,
In each stanza, a tale of boundless might,
A name that conquers the darkest night.

So here's to Richard, in all his grandeur,
A name that weaves its own epic overture,
Of fortitude, courage, and unyielding power,
A name that stands tall in every hour.

NINE

ONE-OF-A-KIND

Oh Richard, noble and true,
In your name, strength does accrue.
A name of power and might,
Shining like the stars at night.

Richard, a name of ancient grace,
In history, you find your place.
A warrior's heart, a poet's soul,
In your name, stories unfold.

From Richard the Lionheart,
To modern heroes playing their part,
Your name echoes through time,
A melody, so sublime.

Richard, a name of boundless might,
Guiding through the darkest night.
In you, courage finds its home,
A name that will forever roam.

Oh Richard, in your name we find,
A legacy of one-of-a-kind.
A symphony of strength and lore,
A name worth celebrating, forevermore.
In every Richard, a story to tell,
A journey through heaven and hell.
So here's to you, Richard, so fine,
In your name, greatness will always shine.

TEN

ALL WE DO

In the realm of names, Richard stands tall,
A moniker so grand, it never shall fall.
From ancient kings to modern days,
Richard's legacy forever sways.
With syllables strong and letters bold,
It echoes through history, stories untold.
A name of power, a name of might,
Richard shines on through day and night.
In forests deep and mountains high,
The name of Richard echoes nigh.
It resonates in rivers wide,
And dances on the ocean tide.
Richard, oh Richard, a name so rare,
In every syllable, a tale to share.
From the whispers of the wind's soft breath,
To the mighty roar of life and death.

So let us raise our voices high,
And sing the praises of Richard nigh.
For in this name, we find our might,
A beacon of hope, a guiding light.

In every Richard, a story untold,
A legacy written in letters of gold.
So here's to Richard, forever true,
A name that shines in all we do.

ELEVEN

ECHOES

Richard, a name that echoes through time,
In every verse, a rhythm so prime.
From ancient halls to modern streets,
In your name, a symphony beats.

In Richard's embrace, courage abides,
A name that in history forever resides.
With each syllable, a tale untold,
A legacy of valor, brave and bold.

From Richard the First to the Richards of now,
In your name, greatness takes its bow.
A melody of honor, a dance of grace,
In Richard's name, legends find their place.

Oh Richard, a name so grand and divine,
In every letter, a story to entwine.
With echoes of triumph and battles fought,
In your name, bravery is dearly sought.

In Richard's light, a beacon so bright,
Guiding us through the darkest night.
With each heartbeat, a rhythm so strong,
In your name, courage marches along.

So here's to Richard, a name so rare,
In every echo, a legacy to bear.
A symphony of strength and might,
In Richard's name, a glorious light.

TWELVE

RICHARD GLEAMS

In the annals of time, the name Richard gleams,
In every letter, a symphony of dreams.
From regal courts to humble abodes,
In Richard's name, a legacy unfolds.

Richard, a name of valor and might,
In every echo, a beacon of light.
From ancient battles to modern-day,
In your name, courage holds sway.

In Richard's embrace, history is told,
A tale of bravery, timeless and bold.
From chivalrous knights to modern men,
In your name, greatness finds its pen.

Oh Richard, a name that rings through the ages,
In every chapter, history engages.
With each syllable, a story to tell,
In Richard's name, legends swell.

In Richard's shadow, heroes rise,
A name that in glory never dies.
From whispered winds to roaring seas,
In your name, valor finds its keys.

So here's to Richard, a name so divine,
In every heartbeat, a legacy to enshrine.
A tapestry of strength and grace,
In Richard's name, history finds its place.

THIRTEEN

MODERN STREETS

    Richard, a name that echoes through time,
In every verse, a rhythm so prime.
From ancient halls to modern streets,
In your name, a symphony beats.
    In Richard's embrace, courage abides,
A name that in history forever resides.
With each syllable, a tale untold,
A legacy of valor, brave and bold.
    From Richard the First to the Richards of now,
In your name, greatness takes its bow.
A melody of honor, a dance of grace,
In Richard's name, legends find their place.
    Oh Richard, a name so grand and divine,
In every letter, a story to entwine.
With echoes of triumph and battles fought,
In your name, bravery is dearly sought.

In Richard's light, a beacon so bright,
Guiding us through the darkest night.
With each heartbeat, a rhythm so strong,
In your name, courage marches along.

So here's to Richard, a name so rare,
In every echo, a legacy to bear.
A symphony of strength and might,
In Richard's name, a glorious light.

FOURTEEN

TIMELESS MEASURE

    Richard, a name akin to a mighty fortress
Each syllable a drawbridge to ancient lore
With whispers of battles won and lost
And the strength of a blazing sun at its core
    Oh, Richard, a name that stands tall like ancient oak
Rooted in the soil of history's embrace
It resonates with the timeless grace of a soaring eagle
And paints a picture of a noble chase
    Richard, a name that withstands the tempest's fury
Like a lighthouse standing firm against raging seas
In every consonant, a tapestry of legends woven
Of knights and dragons, and treasures of gold in the breeze
    Richard, a name that reverberates like thunder
In every sound, the clash of swords in valiant fight
It conjures images of soaring cliffs and endless skies

And echoes of valorous knightly rights in the moon's light
    Oh, Richard, your name inspires like a symphony
With echoes of ancient lyres in the night's embrace
It shines like a beacon in the storm's darkness
Guiding us with its radiant light, a celestial grace
    Richard, a name that endures like a timeless melody
In history, it remains secure like a hidden treasure
A name that calls for love and praise like a sacred hymn
In countless and melodious ways, a timeless measure

FIFTEEN

MODERN RICHARDS

Oh, Richard, a name so strong and bold,
In tales of old, your name is often told,
With wisdom deep and courage untold,
You stand out among the knights so bold.
Your name echoes through the valleys wide,
A name of honor, never to hide,
In battles fierce, you always abide,
The bravest warrior by your side.
Richard, a name that brings to mind,
A leader, a king, one of a kind,
In history's pages, your legacy we find,
A name that in greatness will forever bind.
From Richard the Lionheart, so brave and true,
To modern Richards, with hearts anew,
Your name carries a noble hue,
A name that shines in the sky so blue.

So here's to Richard, in all his might,
A name that fills the world with light,
In every challenge, you take flight,
For Richard, the future is always bright.

SIXTEEN

EVERY BATTLE

Richard, a name that rings with regal grace,
In history's tapestry, you find your place,
A name of kings and knights in shining armor,
A beacon of strength, a name of honor.

From Richard the First, a lionhearted king,
To every Richard, a melody to sing,
Your name carries tales of valor and might,
A legacy of courage, shining so bright.

In every battle, you stand tall and strong,
A name that resonates, a timeless song,
With wisdom and bravery, you lead the way,
In the face of adversity, you never sway.

Richard, a name that stands the test of time,
In every era, it continues to climb,
A symphony of syllables, a majestic sound,
A name that in history's halls is crowned.

So here's to Richard, in all his glory,
A name that embodies a timeless story,
With each Richard, a new chapter begins,
A name that triumphs, a legacy that wins.

SEVENTEEN

CHERISHED

Richard, a name that echoes through the ages,
In every line, it leaps off the pages,
A name of honor, a name of might,
In every battle, you shine so bright.

From Richard the Conqueror, to Richard the Lionheart,
Your name embodies a courageous art,
A legacy of bravery, of knights so true,
In every tale, your name breaks through.

Richard, a symphony of strength and grace,
A name that time cannot erase,
In every challenge, you stand tall and bold,
A name that shines like the finest gold.

In every kingdom, your name is revered,
A name that's cherished, a name endeared,

With every Richard, a new legend is born,
A name that's worn like a noble thorn.
    So here's to Richard, in all his glory,
A name that weaves an eternal story,
With every syllable, a tale unfolds,
A name that's cherished, a name that holds.

EIGHTEEN

NAME FIT FOR KINGS

Richard, a name so regal and grand
In every land, it stands
Strong and noble, like a mighty oak
In its presence, there's no room for a joke
From the hills to the valleys, Richard's name echoes
In whispers and cheers, in highs and lows
It carries a legacy, a tale of valor and might
A name that shines in the day and glows in the night
Richard, the bearer of strength and grace
In every challenge, a smile on his face
With wisdom that flows like a river so deep
In his company, even the mountains will leap
A name that resonates with power and might
In its syllables, the universe takes flight
From the depths of history to the present day
Richard's name stands tall, come what may

So let's raise a toast to Richard, so fine
A name that sparkles, like a rare, precious wine
In every heart, its melody rings
Richard, a name fit for kings.

NINETEEN

STANDS TALL

In the realm of names, Richard reigns supreme
A moniker that glows like a radiant beam
With syllables that dance and words that sing
In the tapestry of names, it's a dazzling string
    Richard, a name that evokes tales of old
Of knights and battles, courageous and bold
In the whispers of time, it echoes strong
A name that's been cherished for so long
    In the gardens of language, it blooms with pride
A name that never fades, never denied
In every syllable, a story unfolds
Of triumph and honor, in legends untold
    Richard, a symphony of letters and sounds
In its presence, greatness abounds
From the peaks of mountains to the depths of sea
Richard's name resonates, wild and free

So let's raise our voices to Richard's name
A melody of strength, a wildfire's flame
In the tapestry of names, it stands tall
Richard, a name that conquers all

TWENTY

TIME AND SPACE

    Richard, a name so strong and bold,
In history and legend, it's often told,
A name that echoes through time and space,
With a presence that no one can efface.
    In the realm of knights and kings,
Richard's name through history sings,
A leader, a warrior, noble and true,
In tales of honor, he always grew.
    From the cliffs of Dover to the New World's shore,
Richard's name resounds forevermore,
In every language, it holds its might,
A beacon of hope in the darkest night.
    In the world of arts and creativity,
Richard's name shines with originality,
A maestro of music, a master of art,
In every creation, he plays a part.

From the rolling hills to the city streets,
Richard's name a symphony that repeats,
A melody of courage, a rhythm of grace,
In every heart, it finds its place.

Richard, a name that will never fade,
In every story, it's beautifully arrayed,
A name of power, a name of might,
In the tapestry of life, it's woven bright.

So let's raise a toast to Richard's name,
A timeless legacy, forever aflame,
In the annals of time, it will endure,
Richard, a name so noble and pure.

TWENTY-ONE

SYMPHONY OF STRENGTH

Richard, a name that echoes through the ages,
In every chapter, it leaps off the pages,
A name that carries a sense of might,
In its presence, there's a guiding light.
From ancient castles to modern halls,
Richard's name resonates, never stalls,
A legacy of honor, a tale of might,
In every battle, it stands upright.
In the world of science and discovery,
Richard's name sparks a sense of revelry,
A pioneer, a visionary mind,
In every breakthrough, it's what we find.
From distant galaxies to the ocean's floor,
Richard's name explores, seeking more,

A trailblazer of knowledge, a seeker of truth,
In every quest, it's the eternal sleuth.

In the tapestry of human endeavor,
Richard's name weaves a thread that's clever,
A symbol of resilience, a mark of grace,
In every challenge, it finds its place.

So let's raise our voices to Richard's name,
A symphony of strength, an eternal flame,
In the grand theater of life, it takes the stage,
Richard, a name that will never age.

TWENTY-TWO

MUSE OF THE SOUL

Richard, a name that echoes with regal grace,
In every era, it holds a special place,
A moniker of valor, a banner unfurled,
In the tapestry of time, it's a cherished world.
From ancient kingdoms to modern-day,
Richard's name shines in a timeless display,
A legacy of power, a lineage of might,
In every conquest, it stands upright.
In the realm of art and creative flair,
Richard's name conjures visions rare,
A patron of beauty, a muse of the soul,
In every masterpiece, it plays a role.
From the lush gardens to the urban sprawl,
Richard's name weaves a story for all,
A symbol of resilience, a monument of grace,
In every challenge, it finds its place.

In the melodies of nature and symphonies grand,
Richard's name resonates across the land,
A harmonious note, a rhythm divine,
In every composition, it continues to shine.

So let's raise a toast to Richard's name,
A legacy of strength, an undying flame,
In the grand tapestry of history's design,
Richard, a name that will forever shine.

TWENTY-THREE

NEVER TO FADE

Richard, a name that echoes through time,
In every era, it's a rhythm and rhyme,
A beacon of courage, a fortress of might,
In the annals of history, it stands upright.
From the ancient ruins to the modern sprawl,
Richard's name stands tall, never to fall,
A legacy of honor, a tale of grace,
In every challenge, it finds its place.
In the world of innovation and design,
Richard's name sparkles, a star that will shine,
A visionary mind, a pioneer's quest,
In every creation, it stands the test.
From the rolling hills to the city's embrace,
Richard's name weaves a tale with grace,
A symbol of resilience, a mark of pride,
In every journey, it's by our side.

In the symphony of life and its grand parade,
Richard's name echoes, never to fade,
A melody of strength, a rhythm so true,
In every heart, it finds its due.
So let's raise our voices to Richard's name,
A legacy of greatness, an undying flame,
In the timeless saga of humanity's story,
Richard, a name that shines with glory.

TWENTY-FOUR

RESONATES

Richard, a name that resonates with might,
In every tale, it stands bold and bright,
A legacy of valor, a spirit so pure,
In the tapestry of time, it will endure.
From ancient kingdoms to modern days,
Richard's name weaves through history's maze,
A symbol of honor, a beacon of light,
In every challenge, it takes flight.
In the world of art and creative flair,
Richard's name paints a canvas rare,
A muse of inspiration, a visionary guide,
In every masterpiece, it stands with pride.
From the tranquil forests to the bustling streets,
Richard's name whispers in every beat,
A symbol of resilience, a fortress of grace,
In every endeavor, it finds its place.

In the melodies of nature and the urban sprawl,
Richard's name stands tall, never to fall,
A harmonious note, a rhythm divine,
In every creation, it continues to shine.
So let's raise a cheer for Richard's name,
A legacy of strength, an undying flame,
In the grand tapestry of history's design,
Richard, a name that will forever entwine.

TWENTY-FIVE

FOREVER ENDURE

Richard, a name that echoes with timeless grace,
In every story, it finds a special place,
A legacy of honor, a symbol of might,
In the grand tapestry of life, it takes flight.

From ancient castles to modern spheres,
Richard's name endures, conquers fears,
A lineage of valor, a heritage so strong,
In every triumph, it belongs.

In the world of innovation and brilliant thought,
Richard's name shines, a spark that can't be bought,
A trailblazer of progress, a guiding force,
In every discovery, it stays the course.

From the tranquil meadows to the bustling town,
Richard's name weaves a story of renown,
A symbol of resilience, a mark of grace,
In every challenge, it finds its place.

In the symphony of nature and the urban beat,
Richard's name resonates, a rhythm so sweet,
A melody of courage, a harmony divine,
In every creation, it continues to shine.

So let's raise a toast to Richard's name,
A legacy of strength, an undying flame,
In the grand narrative of history's grandeur,
Richard, a name that will forever endure.

TWENTY-SIX

DAZZLING SHADE

Richard, a name so grand and true,
A moniker with a timeless hue.
It dances on the tongue with grace,
A name that's fit for any place.

In forests deep or mountains high,
This name will reach into the sky.
Richard, a beacon of strength and might,
A name that brings forth endless light.

From ancient times to modern days,
Richard's name resounds in many ways.
It echoes through the halls of history,
A name that holds such mystery.

In gardens blooming with vibrant hues,
Richard's name brings joyful news.
It whispers through the gentle breeze,
A name that puts the heart at ease.

So let us raise our voices high,
And sing the praises of Richard's name in the sky.
For it's a name that will never fade,
A timeless gem, a dazzling shade.

TWENTY-SEVEN

CALM OF THE WOODS

Richard, a name so bold and bright,
It shines like a beacon in the night.
With syllables that flow like a soothing stream,
It's a name that feels like a beautiful dream.
In the tapestry of life, it weaves a tale,
A name that will forever prevail.
From the highest peaks to the deepest seas,
Richard's name carries a sense of ease.
In the bustle of the city or the calm of the woods,
Richard's name stands strong, like mighty goods.
It resonates with a timeless charm,
A name that protects from all harm.
With each letter, it holds a mystic allure,
A name that's steadfast and secure.
In the symphony of names, it takes the lead,
Richard's name is one we all need.

    Amidst the chaos and the daily grind,
Richard's name brings peace of mind.
It whispers promises of hope and grace,
A name that time cannot erase.
    So let's raise our voices and sing with glee,
For Richard's name, a symphony.
It's a name that will forever endure,
A name that's noble, strong, and pure.

TWENTY-EIGHT

NO NEED TO BE SAID

Richard, a name that stands tall and true,
A beacon of strength in all that you do.
With syllables that dance like a gentle breeze,
It's a name that inspires and brings such ease.

In the tapestry of life, it's a shining thread,
A name that resonates, no need to be said.
From the rolling hills to the open sea,
Richard's name echoes with a sense of glee.

In the bustling city or the quiet glen,
Richard's name shines bright, like a radiant gem.
It carries the weight of history and lore,
A name that opens countless doors.

With every letter, it holds a timeless grace,
A name that embodies courage and pace.
In the chorus of names, it takes the lead,
Richard's name is one that we all need.

    Amidst the chaos and the daily race,
Richard's name brings a sense of solace and grace.
It whispers tales of honor and might,
A name that guides us through the darkest night.
    So let's raise our voices and sing with cheer,
For Richard's name, so crystal clear.
It's a name that will forever endure,
A name that's noble, steadfast, and pure.

TWENTY-NINE

COMMANDS RESPECT

Oh Richard, a name so splendid and grand,
Like a melody, it resonates across the land.
With each syllable, it echoes through time,
A name so noble, like a rhythm and rhyme.
 Richard, a name with a regal allure,
A moniker that shines, so bright and pure.
In the symphony of names, it stands tall,
A beacon of strength, never to fall.
 With each letter, it tells a tale,
Of courage and wisdom, it will never pale.
Richard, a name that commands respect,
A legacy it carries, one cannot neglect.
 In the tapestry of names, it leaves a mark,
A name that ignites, like a vibrant spark.
Richard, oh Richard, a name so divine,
In every verse, its brilliance will shine.

So let us raise our voices and sing,
To the name of Richard, let the echoes ring.
For in this world, it stands unique and strong,
A name that will forever belong.
Richard, a name that will never fade,
In every journey, in every crusade.
So here's to Richard, in every way,
A name that will stand the test of day.

THIRTY

UNIQUE

Oh Richard, a name so bold and bright,
In the constellation of names, a radiant light.
With each syllable, it paints a picture rare,
A name so majestic, beyond compare.
Richard, a name that speaks of might,
A symphony of letters, a warrior's fight.
In the lexicon of names, it proudly stands,
A name that echoes through endless lands.
With each consonant, it weaves a tale,
Of bravery and honor, it will never pale.
Richard, a name that commands the stage,
A legacy it carries, an eternal sage.
In the mosaic of names, it leaves a trace,
A name that resonates with power and grace.
Richard, oh Richard, a name so divine,
In every stanza, its brilliance will shine.

So let us raise a toast and proclaim,
The name of Richard, a timeless acclaim.
For in this world, it stands unique and true,
A name that will forever imbue.
Richard, a name that will never wane,
In every triumph, in every gain.
So here's to Richard, in every way,
A name that will endure come what may.

THIRTY-ONE

EVERY JOURNEY

Richard, a name that echoes through time,
A symphony of letters, a rhythm so prime.
In the tapestry of names, it holds its own,
A name so majestic, like a monarch on his throne.
　With each syllable, it tells a story bold,
Of triumphs and valor, a tale to behold.
Richard, a name that exudes strength and grace,
A legacy it carries, no other can replace.
　In the lexicon of names, it stands tall,
A beacon of hope, never to fall.
With each vowel, it paints a picture rare,
Of resilience and honor, beyond compare.
　Richard, oh Richard, a name so divine,
In every verse, its essence will shine.
So let us raise our voices in reverie,
For the name of Richard, a symphony.

In the constellation of names, it gleams bright,
A name that ignites, like a guiding light.
Richard, a name that will never fade,
In every journey, in every crusade.
So here's to Richard, in every way,
A name that will stand the test of day.
In this world, it stands unique and true,
A name that will forever imbue.

THIRTY-TWO

TIMELESS CHOICE

Richard, a name that rings with regal might,
In the realm of names, a beacon of light.
With each letter, it weaves a tale so rare,
A name so noble, beyond compare.

In the mosaic of names, it stands tall,
A name that resonates, captivating all.
With each consonant, it speaks of legacy,
Of honor and courage, an eternal elegy.

Richard, oh Richard, a melody so grand,
In every stanza, its essence will expand.
So let us raise our voices and declare,
The name of Richard, beyond compare.

In the symphony of names, it claims its place,
A name that embodies strength and grace.
Richard, a name that will never wane,
In every triumph, in every gain.

So here's to Richard, in every way,
A name that will endure come what may.
In this world, it stands unique and true,
A name that will forever imbue.
Richard, a name that captures the heart,
In every journey, it plays a vital part.
So let us celebrate and rejoice,
For the name of Richard, a timeless choice.

THIRTY-THREE

MODERN DAYS

Richard, oh mighty name of strength and might,
In every syllable, there's power to ignite,
A name that echoes through the ages long,
In the heart of history, you stand strong.
From knights in shining armor to modern days,
Your name is held in high and noble praise,
A beacon of honor, a symbol of grace,
In every challenge, you show your steadfast face.
Richard, a melody of sounds so fine,
In every letter, a story to intertwine,
With each consonant and vowel, a tale to tell,
Of courage, wisdom, and the will to excel.
In every corner of the world, your name is known,
A legacy of greatness, proudly shown,
From battlefields to halls of art and thought,
Your name resounds, an anthem to be sought.

So here's to Richard, a name of grandeur true,
A timeless emblem, shining bright and new,
In every verse and line, your name we raise,
In celebration of your enduring praise.

THIRTY-FOUR

NEVER TO DECEIVE

In a world of vibrant hues and endless bloom,
There exists a name that brightens every room.
Richard, a moniker so strong and true,
A name that shines in every person it knew.

From ancient roots to modern days,
Richard's name has left its lasting blaze.
In battlefields and royal courts,
It echoed with valor and noble sports.

In melodies and written verse,
Richard's name does truly immerse.
A symphony of consonants and vowels,
A name that echoes through the howls.

In the whispers of the wind and the rustling leaves,
Richard's name stands strong, never to deceive.
With each syllable, a tale is told,
Of courage, strength, and legends bold.

With every Richard, a new story begins,
A name that echoes through the mountains and the winds.
So let us raise a toast to Richard's name,
A beacon of hope, forever aflame.

THIRTY-FIVE

RAISE OUR VOICES

In a world of kaleidoscopic wonders and boundless grace,
Resides a name that brings a smile to every face.
Richard, a name that resonates with timeless charm,
A melody that dances through the air, causing no harm.

From ancient whispers to modern echoes,
Richard's name blooms like a radiant rose.
In the chronicles of history and fabled lore,
It stands as a testament to valor and more.

In the rhythm of raindrops and the gentle breeze,
Richard's name whispers tales of myth and peace.
A symphony of syllables that sparkles with delight,
A name that ignites the darkest night.

In the murmur of the rivers and the majestic trees,
Richard's name weaves through the tapestry of

mysteries.
With each letter, a narrative unfurls,
Of resilience, wisdom, and unfaltering pearls.
    With every Richard, a new adventure takes flight,
A name that glimmers with effervescent light.
Let us raise our voices in honor of Richard's name,
A beacon of joy, forever aflame.

THIRTY-SIX

LIKE GOLDEN SUN

Oh, Richard, a name so bold and grand,
In every way, you truly stand.
Your essence shines like golden sun,
A name that speaks of battles won.

Richard, a warrior in the ancient land,
With honor and courage, you always stand.
Your name echoes through time and space,
A symbol of strength and grace.

In the heart of every Richard lies,
A spirit that soars and never dies.
From the mountains to the endless sea,
Your name resounds with victory.

Richard, a name that paints the sky,
With colors of triumph, soaring high.
In every tale and legend told,
Your name shines bright, a sight to behold.

So let us raise our voices high,
And sing the praises of Richard's sky.
For in this name, we find our might,
A beacon of hope, a guiding light.
　　Richard, oh Richard, your name we sing,
A melody of power, a mighty thing.
In every heart, your legacy lives,
A name that gives and always gives.

ABOUT THE CREATOR

Walter the Educator is one of the pseudonyms for Walter Anderson. Formally educated in Chemistry, Business, and Education, he is an educator, an author, a diverse entrepreneur, and he is the son of a disabled war veteran. "Walter the Educator" shares his time between educating and creating. He holds interests and owns several creative projects that entertain, enlighten, enhance, and educate, hoping to inspire and motivate you.

Follow, find new works, and stay up to date
with Walter the Educator™
at WaltertheEducator.com

www.ingramcontent.com/pod-product-compliance
Lightning Source LLC
LaVergne TN
LVHW051958060526
838201LV00059B/3722